Introduction

Situated on the banks of the River Thames, in the heart of Westminster, the Houses of Parliament are the seat of national government for the United Kingdom.

centuries saw London expanding at an incredible rate both in terms of buildings and population. By 1800, over a million people were living in the city and by 1900 this figure had risen to over six million. New bridges were built across the Thames, at Westminster in 1750 and Blackfriars in 1769. As the city expanded ever outward, the old Roman wall that had stood for centuries was torn down to allow traffic easier access to the city and areas that had once been outlying villages, such as Islington in the north and Battersea in the south, were swallowed up to become part of the now sprawling metropolis.

With size came grinding poverty in some areas, compounded by the age-old problem of sanitation, and crime was also rife on the streets. To answer at least one of these problems, in 1829 Sir Robert Peel created the Metropolitan Police Force in an attempt to establish law and order in the city. The officers were soon nicknamed "Peelers" or "Bobbies" for their founder (the latter remaining in common parlance to this day). Then, in the mid-nineteenth century, the problem of sanitation in London was finally addressed when Joseph Bazalgette oversaw the construction of underground sewers to carry the waste generated in London away from the city. Up until this time the river Thames had been the repository for much of the city's waste and was consequently little more than an open sewer. Following the opening of Bazalgette's sewers the incidences of disease, particularly cholera, in the city were greatly reduced.

As London entered the twentieth century, it was the thriving hub of an empire that stretched across the globe. The optimism

Roman Foundations to Tudor London:
43 AD–1557

This statue of Boudicea, who led the native revolt against the Romans, by Thomas Thornycroft, sits on the western side of Westminster Bridge, near the Houses of Parliament.

LEFT: Traitor's Gate is one of the most famous attractions at the Tower; Edward I had it built to provide an entrance to the tower via the River Thames. Among the many prisoners to have entered the tower through Traitor's Gate are Anne Boleyn and the future Elizabeth I.

LEFT: During the Medieval Ages, London was effectively run by the various guilds that controlled commerce in the city. Although each guild had its own hall there was also a common meeting place, Guildhall, which was built between 1411 and 1440. The building survives to this day following restoration work carried out after bomb damage sustained during World War II.

LEFT: An eighteenth century picture of the buildings and grounds of Hampton Court, which was intended to serve as a riverside retreat for Cardinal Wolsey, the Archbishop of York during the reign of Henry VIII. However, in a bid to curry favor with the monarch Wolsey presented it to Henry in 1528. The palace was opened to the public in 1838 by Queen Victoria and remains a popular tourist destination to this day. One of the most popular attractions for visitors to Hampton Court is the famous hedge maze that was planted in the gardens in 1702.

RIGHT: This image shows the Tudor gatehouse of St. James's Palace in Pall Mall. The palace was built by Henry VIII between 1531 and 1536 and served as a royal residence for over 300 years. Although it has been the official residence of the monarch since Queen Victoria's time, the reigning sovereigns have preferred to live at Buckingham Palace.

A view of the Georgian section of Hampton Court Palace with a section of the beautiful, formal gardens in the foreground.

LEFT: This astronomical clock at Hampton Court dates from 1528. As well as showing the date and time the clock also depicts the time of high water at London Bridge.

LEFT: Originally built in 1631 by the Dutch merchant Samuel Fortrey, Kew Palace (in the grounds of what is now Kew Gardens) was purchased by George III in 1781 and went on to become a royal residence.

RIGHT: Also in the grounds of Kew, this cottage was given to Queen Charlotte as a wedding gift when she married George III and is known as Queen Charlotte's Cottage. Queen Victoria gifted the cottage to the nation, along with 37 acres of surrounding land, during her Diamond Jubilee in 1897.

LEFT: Another of Inigo Jones's masterpieces, Queens Chapel on Marlborough Road, was commissioned in 1623 by Charles I for his French wife, Henrietta Maria. Originally, the chapel was part of St. James's Palace, but following a fire in 1809 which destroyed the apartments that connected it to the palace and the construction of Marlborough Road in the 1850s it became separate from the palace.

RIGHT: Originally intended as a home for James I's wife, Anne of Denmark, Queen's House in Greenwich was completed in 1637. Unfortunately, Anne died before the house was finished, however it did become a favorite of Henrietta Maria, wife of Charles I. Following Henrietta's death, the house fell out of royal usage and more recently it has been opened as an art gallery displaying works from the collection of the National Maritime Museum.

LEFT: The George Inn on Borough High Street is the only surviving example of the galleried coaching inns that were once common in London. The inn was rebuilt in 1676 following a fire that devastated the Southwark area. It is now owned by the National Trust and operates as a restaurant.

RIGHT: British Prime Minister Tony Blair addressing the media outside No. 10 Downing Street following his victory in the 2005 elections. Only four of the houses built by Sir George Downing following his purchase of the land in 1680 remain. Number ten has been the official residence of the British Prime Minister since 1732, when it was given to the then incumbent Sir Robert Walpole by George II.

LEFT: The Guards Memorial, situated opposite Horse Guards Parade, was designed by Gilbert Ledward and erected in 1926 in memory of the five Foot Guards regiments of the First World War.

RIGHT: A more recent view of Horse Guards Parade; the ultra-modern London Eye can be seen overlooking the building.

LEFT: Westminster Bridge in the eighteenth century; this picture shows the River Thames thronging with busy river traffic.

LEFT: The Great Conservatory in Syon Park was commissioned in 1826 by Third Duke of Northumberland to display his collection of exotic plants. The grandiose structure acted as an inspiration to Joseph Paxton when he was designing the Crystal Palace.

RIGHT: At the time of its construction in 1821, Millbank Prison was the largest penal establishment in London. All that remains of this grim building is a buttress by the Thames that bears a blue plaque with the inscription "Near this site stood Millbank Prison which was opened in 1816 and closed in 1890. This buttress stood at the head of the river steps from which, until 1867, prisoners sentenced to transportation embarked on their journey to Australia."

THE GREAT WORLD OF LONDON.

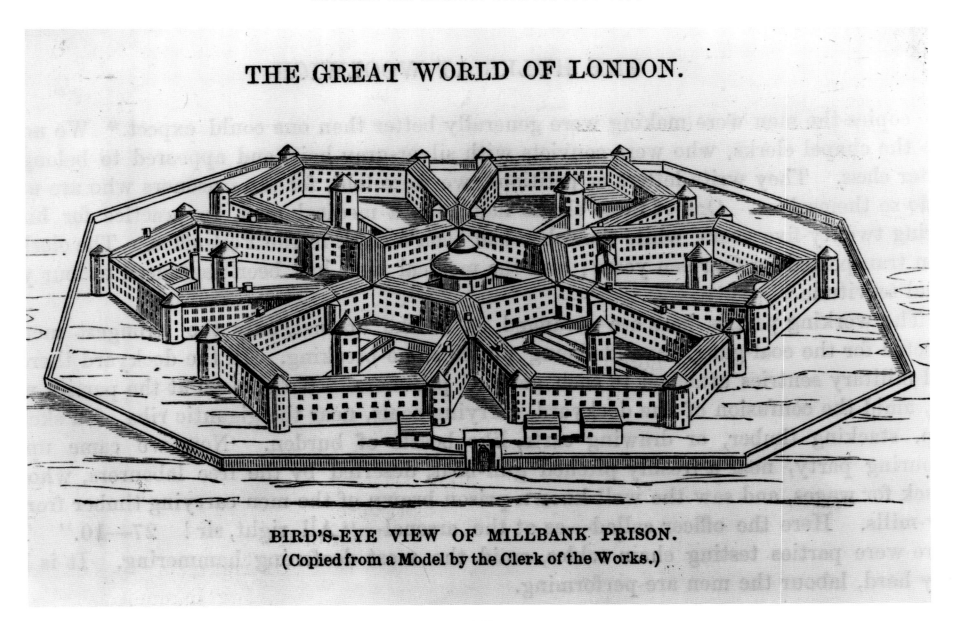

BIRD'S-EYE VIEW OF MILLBANK PRISON.
(Copied from a Model by the Clerk of the Works.)

LEFT: In 1799, a competition was held for designs to replace the Medieval London Bridge that had been decaying for years. The engineer John Rennie won the competition and the bridge he designed is seen here on the occasion of its opening in August 1831. In 1968, the bridge was sold to the American entrepreneur Robert McCulloch who had it shipped to the U.S. where it was rebuilt at Lake Havasu City, Arizona.

FOLLOWING PAGE: London's most elegant bridge, the Albert Bridge is also the only central London bridge that has never been replaced. Despite being strengthened over the years the bridge still bears a plaque at each end that reads, "All troops must break step when marching over this bridge" as it was thought that marching troops from the nearby Chelsea Barracks could cause the bridge structural damage.

LEFT: Although the oldest part of the Houses of Parliament (Westminster Hall) dates to 1097, the Gothic Revival structure that we know today was built between 1834 and 1870 following a fire that almost completely destroyed the old Palace of Westminster. The architect Sir Charles Barry, assisted by Augustus Welby Pugin, designed the new buildings, and one of the most famous features is the clock tower referred to as "Big Ben." In fact Big Ben is the name of the huge bell that was hung in the tower in 1858 and not the tower itself.

One of the great feats of engineering during Victorian times was the construction of the iron and glass Crystal Palace that was built in Hyde Park to house the Great Exhibition of 1851. Following the exhibition, the Crystal Palace was taken down and reconstructed at Sydenham Hill in South London where it remained until it was destroyed by a fire in 1936.

LEFT: Originally known as the West of London and Westminster Cemetery, Brompton Cemetery was opened in 1840. Designed by Benjamin Baud, it is considered one of the best examples of Victorian Metropolitan cemeteries in England.

RIGHT: The front façade of Victoria Station; opened in 1862, Victoria is the third busiest railway station in London after Waterloo and Liverpool Street.

LEFT: One of London's most famous landmarks is Nelson's Column in the heart of Trafalgar Square. The monument was designed by William Railton and built between 1840 and 1843 to commemorate Admiral Horatio Nelson who died during the Battle of Trafalgar in 1805.

RIGHT: Two of the four bronze lions that sit on granite plinths guarding the base of Nelson's Column; unveiled in 1868, the lions were sculpted by Sir Edwin Landseer and cast by Carlo Marocchetti.

LEFT: The original fountain in Trafalgar Square was added in 1845. The remodeled fountain by Sir Edwin Lutyens, seen here, features bronze mermen and mermaids alongside dolphins was unveiled in 1939.

RIGHT: The current Royal Exchange building is the third to house the exchange that was founded by Sir Thomas Gresham in 1566. The previous two buildings were both destroyed by fire; the first in the Great Fire of 1666 and the second in 1838. The third building was designed by Sir William Tite and was officially opened by Queen Victoria in 1844. Currently, the Royal Exchange houses an upmarket shopping center.

LEFT: Sir Robert Smirke designed the main part of the British Museum in 1823, though it took until 1852 for construction of the buildings to be completed. The museum houses a wealth of artifacts from across the globe, the most famous being the Elgin Marbles from the Athenian Parthenon that were brought to Britain in 1806 by Thomas Bruce the seventh Earl of Elgin.

RIGHT: The Victoria and Albert Museum was founded in 1852 as the Museum of Manufacturers and was originally located in Marlborough House. It moved to its current location in 1857 and Sir Aston Webb designed the building that now houses the museum in 1899, the same year that it's name was changed to the Victoria and Albert Museum. The museum is dedicated to the decorative arts.

RIGHT: The original Hungerford Bridge was designed by Isambard Kingdom Brunel and opened 1845 as a pedestrian bridge. In 1859 the Southern Eastern Railway bought it so that they could extend the railway line to Charing Cross. The new bridge opened in 1864. In 2002 two pedestrian bridges were added to the structure and named the Golden Jubilee Bridges in honour of Queen Elizabeth's Golden Jubilee that year. The combined Hungerford and Golden Jubilee bridges provide the only mixed rail and pedestrian crossing in London.

RIGHT: Built on land that had previously been the site of a prison, Tate Britain opened in 1897 as the National Gallery of British Art. The art collector and sugar tycoon Henry Tate paid for the building and also donated his own collection to the gallery after which it became popularly known as the Tate Gallery. This name was officially endorsed in 1932, and since the opening of Tate Modern in 2000 it has been known as Tate Britain. The gallery is home to the largest collection of British art in the world.

The Scotsman William Patterson established the Bank of England in 1694. Originally, it was located in Cheapside and later moved to Princess Street. In 1734, it moved to its present location on Threadneedle Street. Sir Herbert Baker constructed the current building between 1925 and 1939.

The Art Deco influenced Southgate Station on the Piccadilly Line section of the London Underground was designed by Charles Holden and opened on March 13, 1933. It is the most well known of the many Art Deco underground stations that were built around this time.

Battersea Power Station, seen here on the right
overlooking the new developments on the south bank of
the River Thames, was built in 1939 but ceased
electricity generation in 1983. With its four iconic white
chimneys, it has become one of the most recognizable
London landmarks and even featured on the cover of
rock band Pink Floyd's "Animals" album

LEFT AND RIGHT: The 1948 Olympics, held in London, were the first to be held after the Second World War (the 1944 Olympics having been awarded to London in 1939 but cancelled due to the war). These two images show the opening ceremony held at Wembley Stadium and the lighting of the Olympic flame.

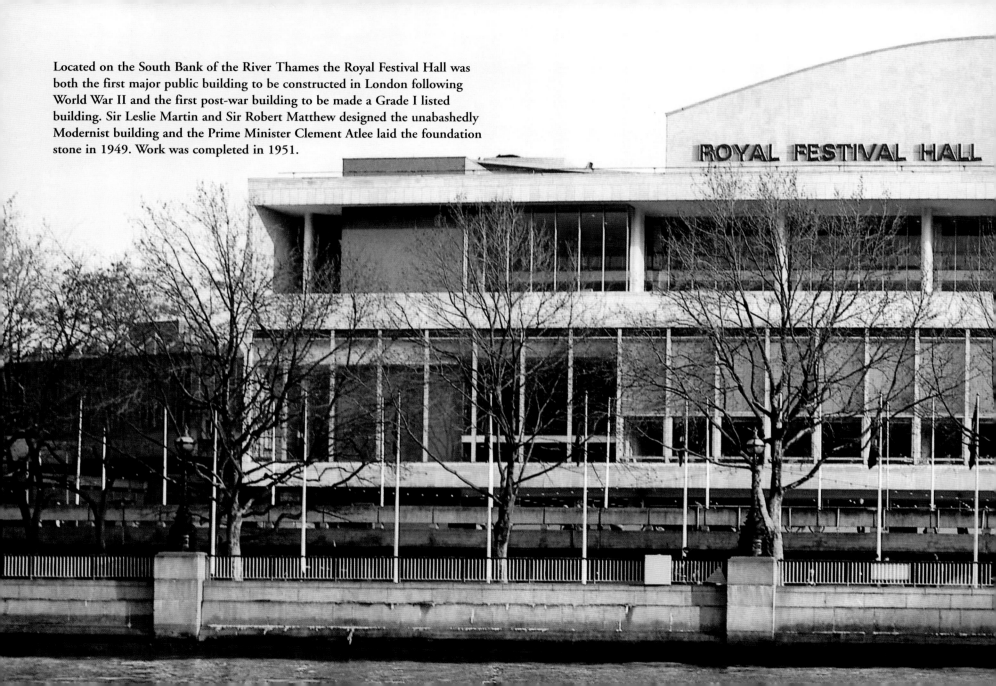

Located on the South Bank of the River Thames the Royal Festival Hall was both the first major public building to be constructed in London following World War II and the first post-war building to be made a Grade I listed building. Sir Leslie Martin and Sir Robert Matthew designed the unabashedly Modernist building and the Prime Minister Clement Atlee laid the foundation stone in 1949. Work was completed in 1951.

ROYAL FESTIVAL HALL